CLOUDS OF MIND

LIFE'S NATURAL BEAUTY

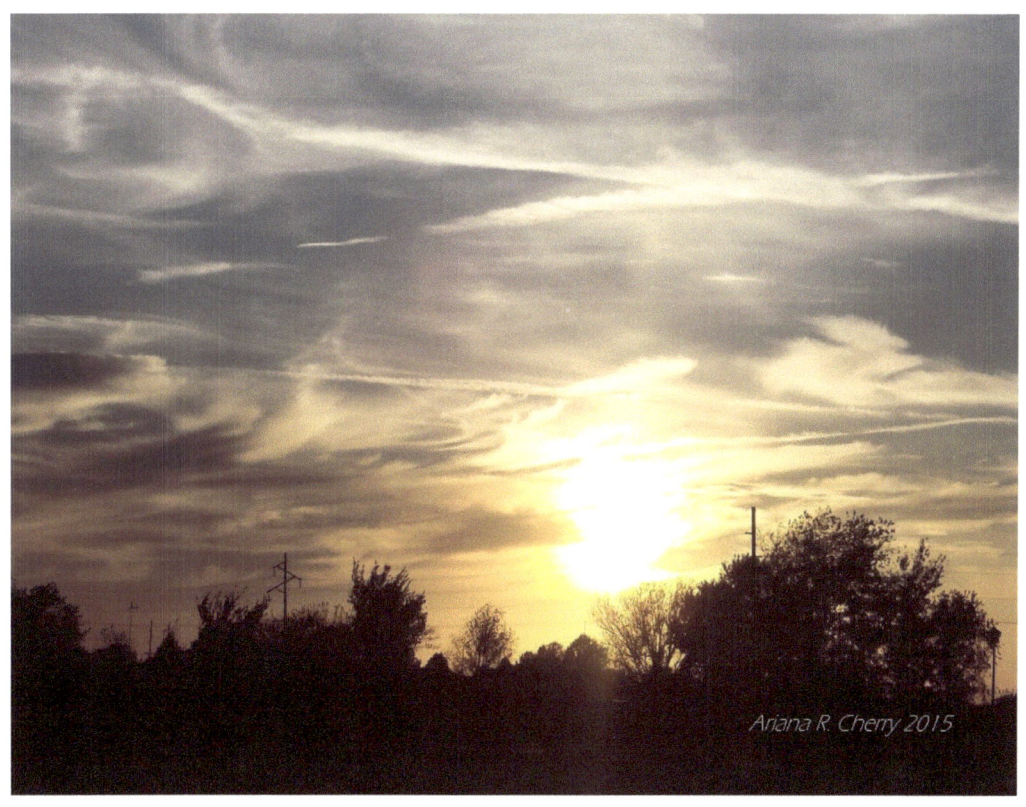

Beauty is all around you. Sometimes, it is okay to have your head in the clouds...*literally.*

ARIANA R CHERRY

This is a collection depicting moments in which I had my head in the clouds... Created, just for you. A collaboration of beauty in our earth's natural paintings and a few words from my own creation too.

Clouds of Mind

Life's Natural Beauty

Ariana R. Cherry

Copyright 2015

Cherry House Publishing

Published in the United States of America

1st Edition

ISBN-13: **978-1519669032**
ISBN-10: **1519669038**

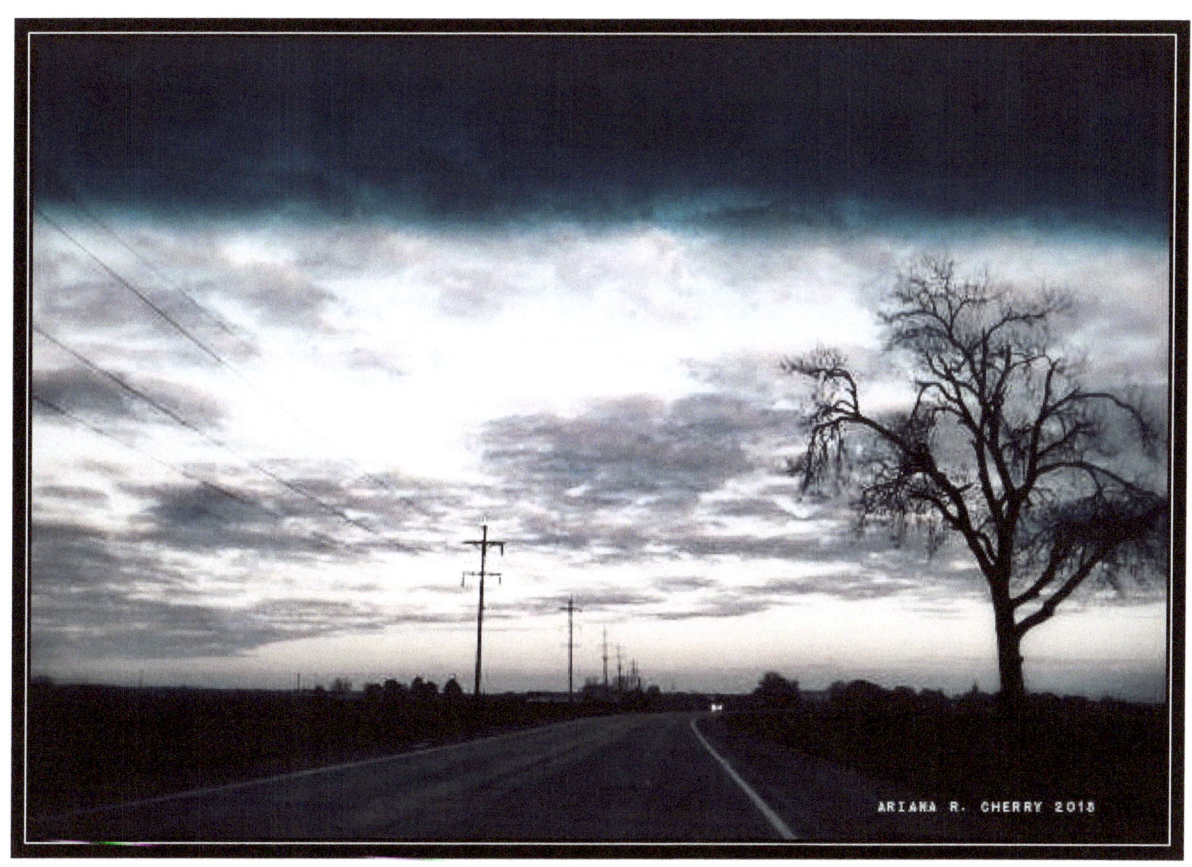

What road are you taking in life?... Will you go happily into the sunset

or ride the open road– and journey on life's curves...?

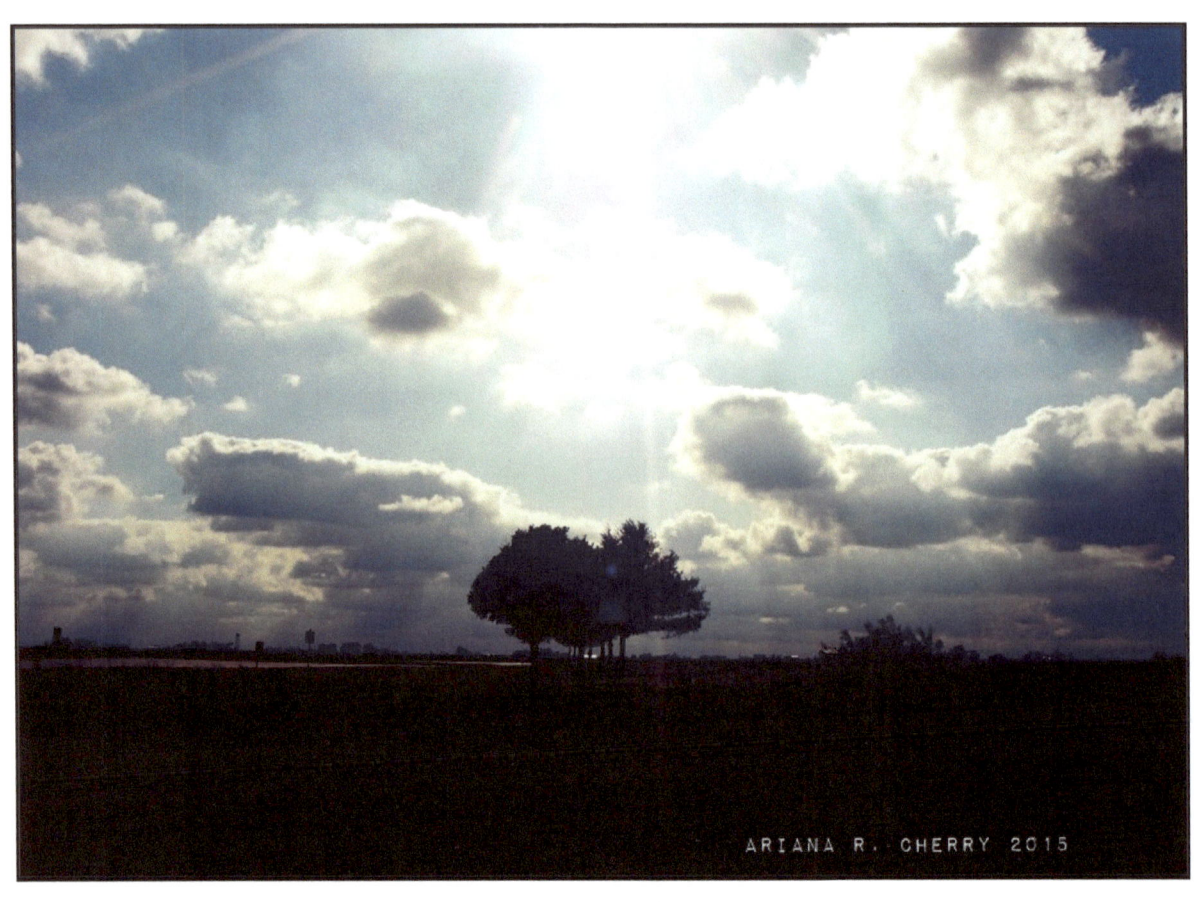

ARIANA R. CHERRY 2015

Sometimes, we need a place to call our own.

A place to hide, collect out thoughts and be inspired...

That place is under the sunlight...

under the clouds, somewhere soft to catch

us when we fall.

And when we are ready to come back,

the sun will guide us home.

        Until we need to escape again.

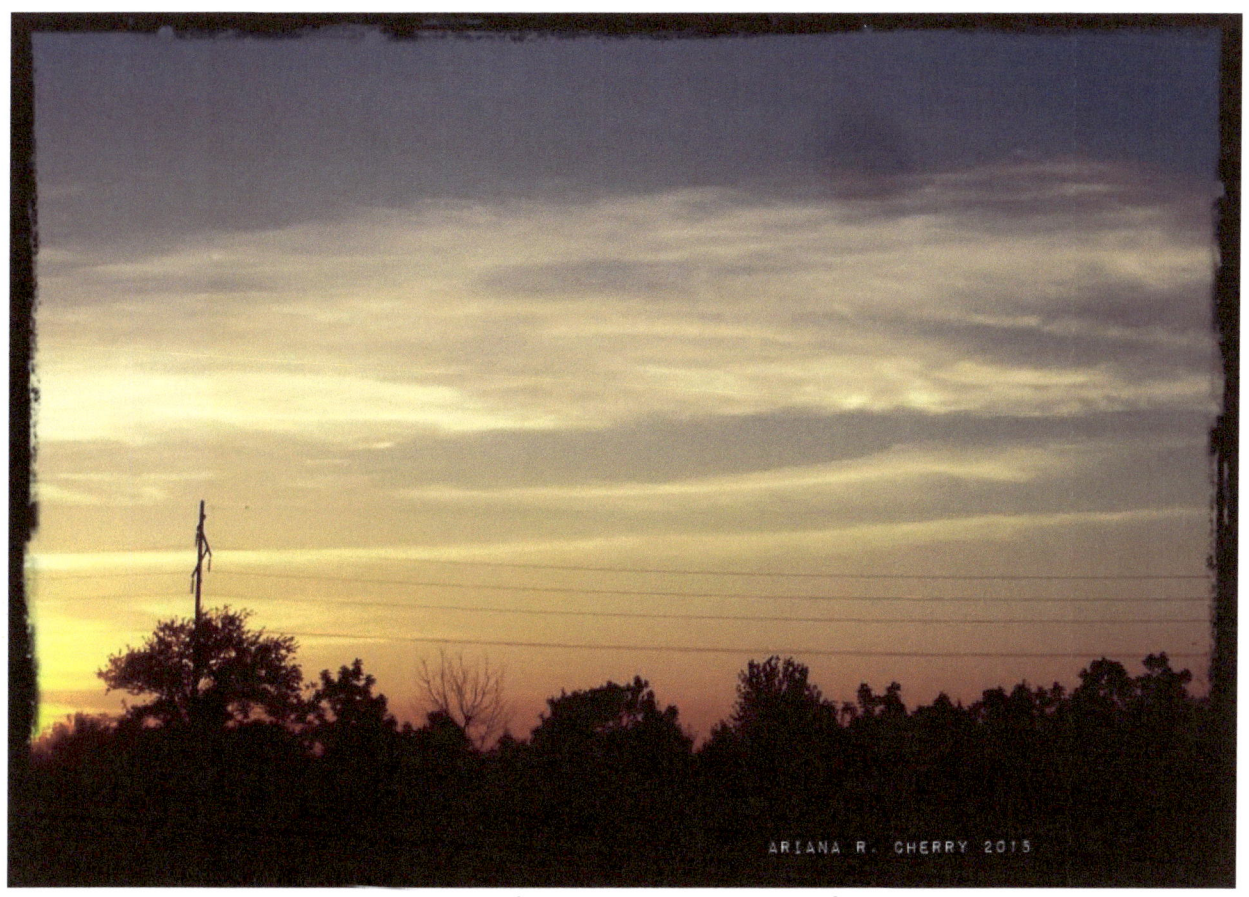

Sunsets are epic. They are the end of a day,

but also mean, you conquered too.

It is also the start, of an evening, filled with hope

and a peace into the darkness

As we wait for the stars to shine their light,

A reminder that we are never... alone in this vast universe.

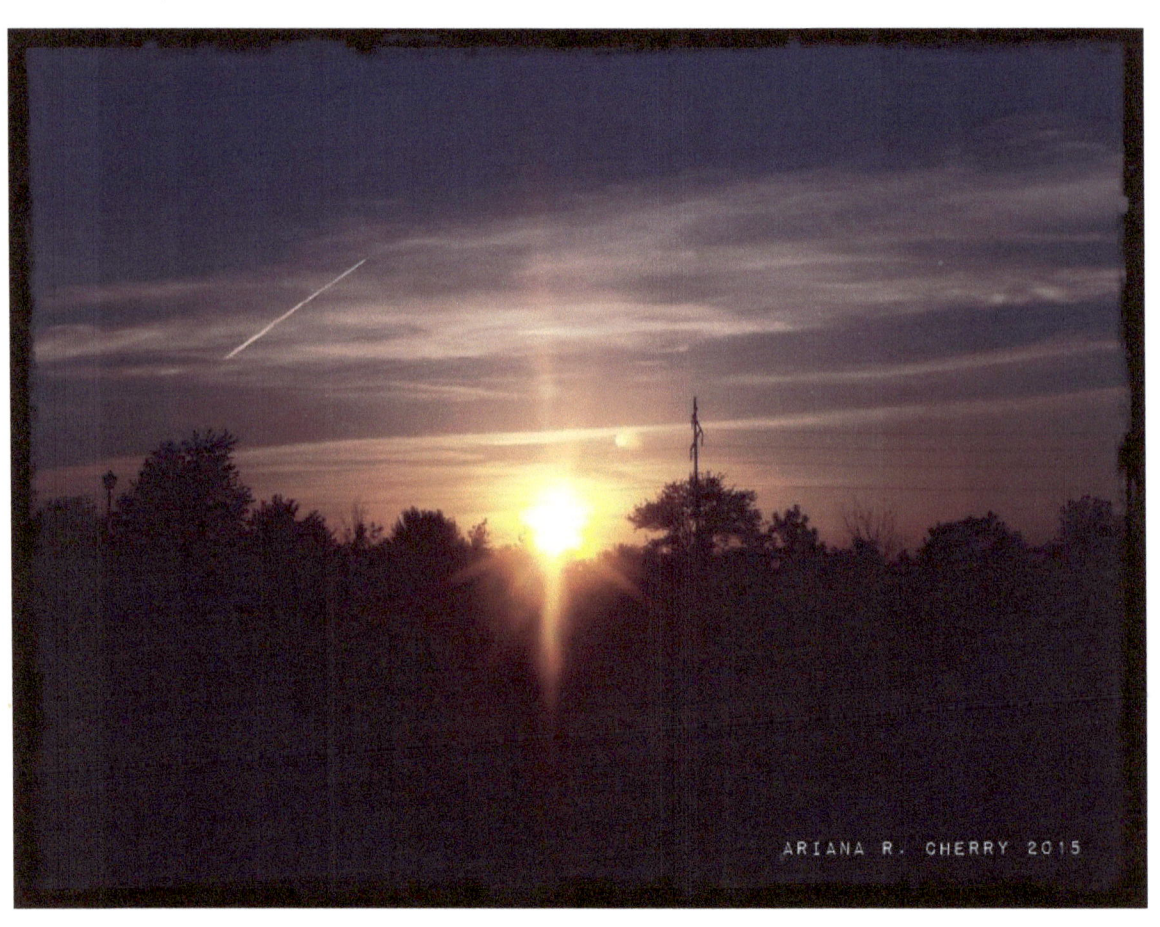

The suns rays reach out to warm us and lead the way.

Often they seem quite blinding, but it's only because they

were created from a love, so strong,

that even we as humans, can't even fathom...

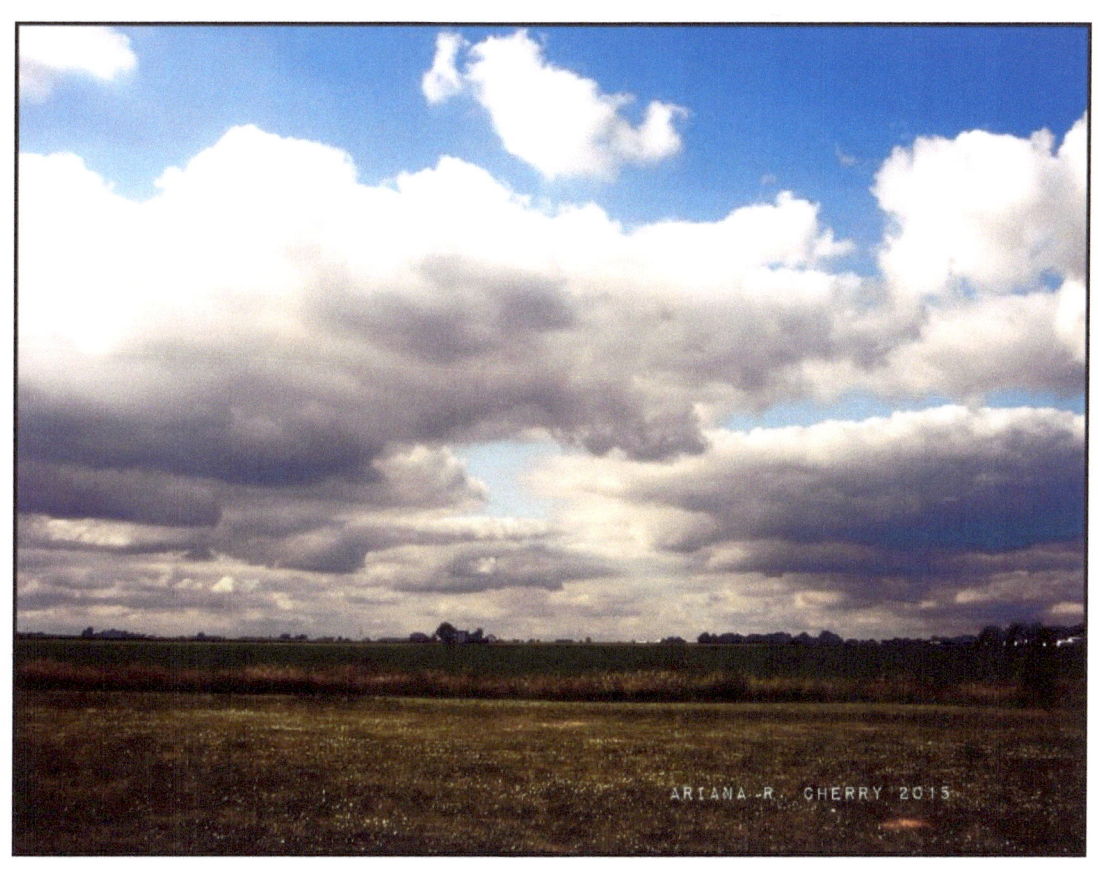

A field of glory, a sky of dreams

and a heart full of hope.

This is where we run to be free

And escape the harshness of the world.

When there's open land, there's an open mind...

And a chance to explore.

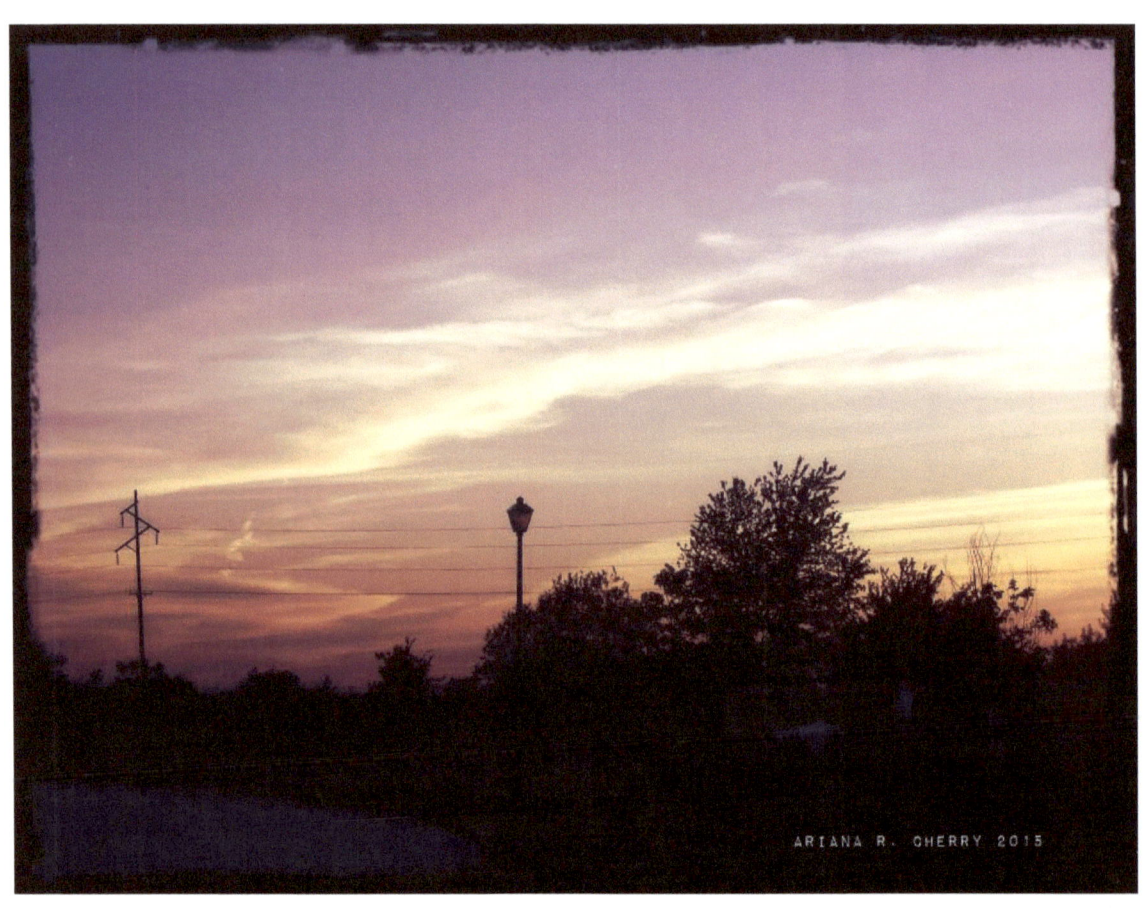

There's a beauty right after sunset.

A peace that is heard right after the sun falls.

Somewhere hidden in the trees, the sunlight fades...
to restore itself to bring inspiration into the next day.

You are never alone from its warmth...

Just look up.

It's there...even if you can't see it.

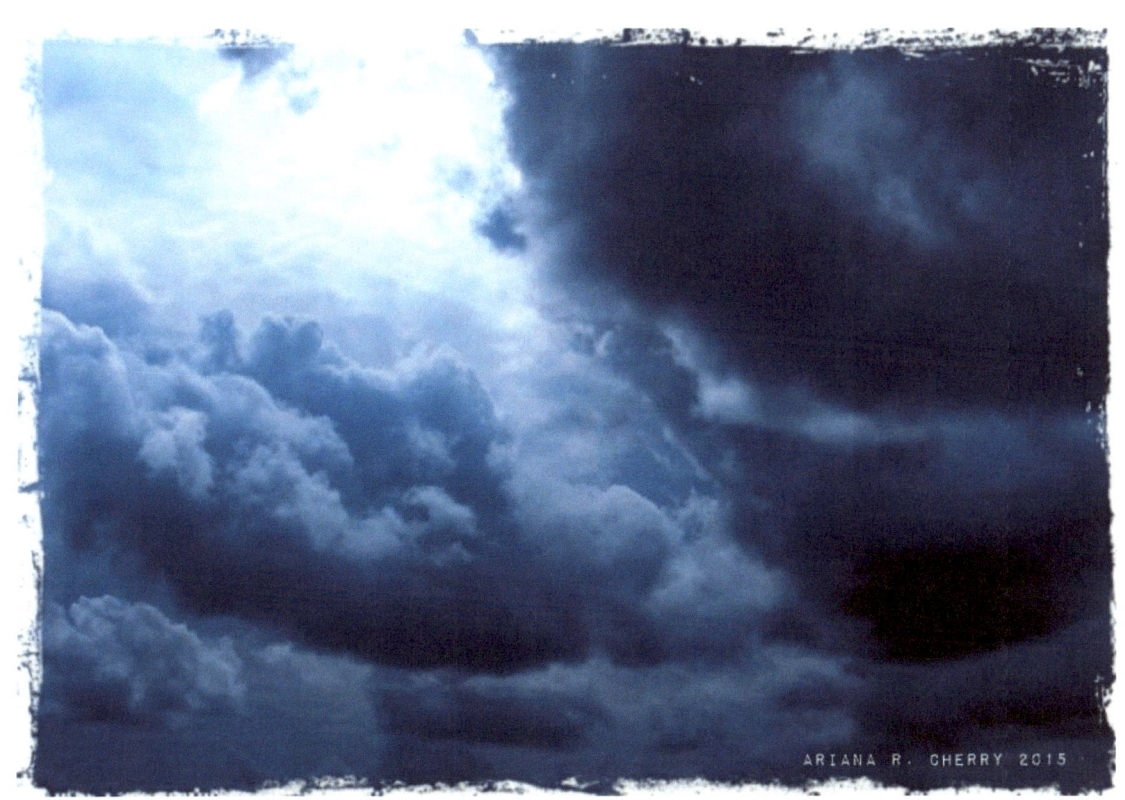

ARIANA R. CHERRY 2015

Life has many storms...

It is full of tests that make us question ourselves
and other times, the outcomes enlighten our spirit.
Life is a classroom and it is all about learning.
We are constantly evolving into the person
whom we were supposed to become....

Everyone has a purpose and a path
Nobody has any room to judge who we are
or the lives that we live.

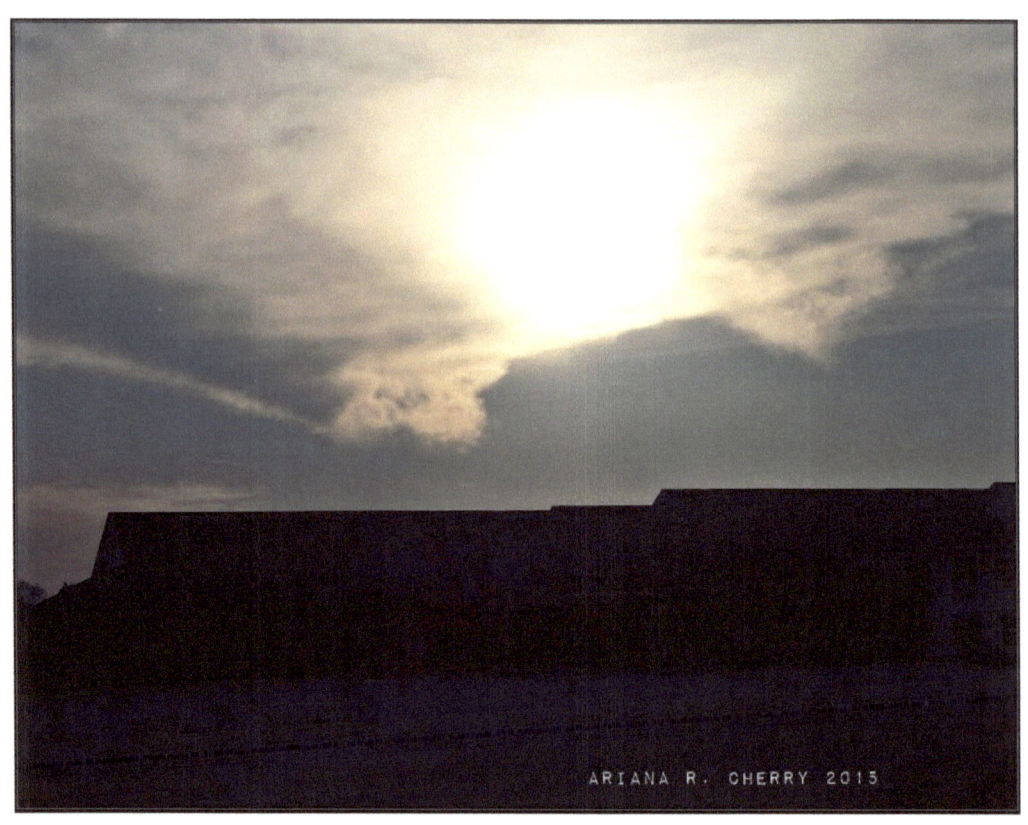

ARIANA R. CHERRY 2013

There are little details in life that act as reminders or
signs to show us, that some higher power is out there.
Events don't happen by accident. There is always a reason.

And sometimes, a piece of beauty,
brightens our linen of vision, to let us know,
that someone is out there listening...
watching and reminding us...**WE ARE LOVED.**

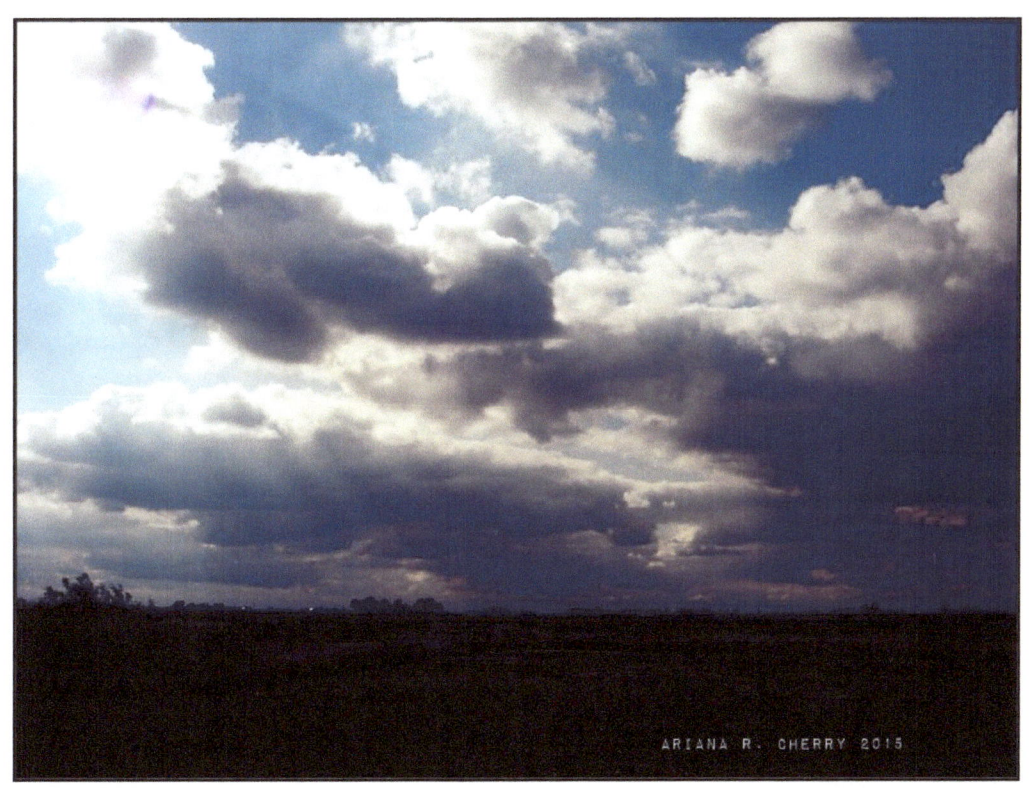

Have you ever looked above in the sky-just for a minute?

Looked up from your phone... from your music...
and just witnessed the peace of silence and
the beauty of the moment?

Have you witnessed the creation – the gift- that we have been given?

Take a moment

Look up

Listen and see the message written in the skies.

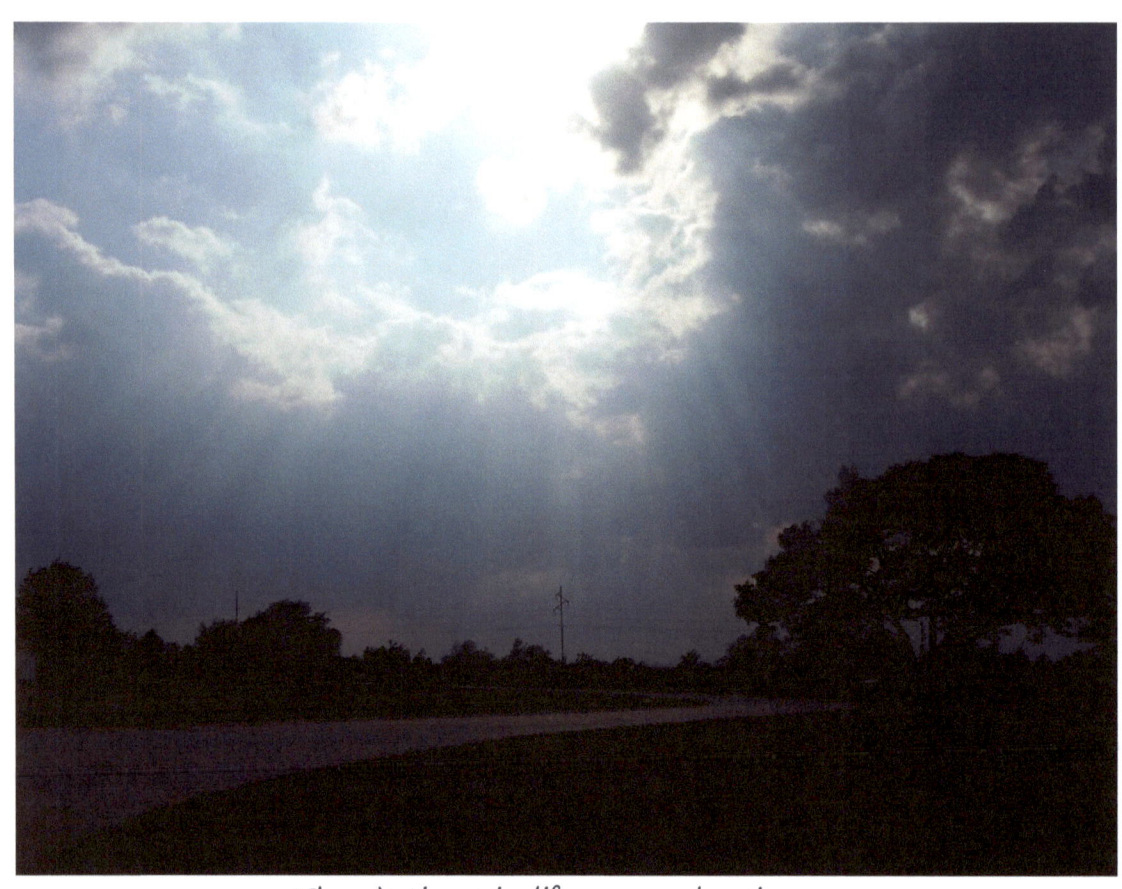

There's times in life we need a sign...

A reminder that we are not alone.

The messages are written in the sky.

While the afterlife isnt necessarily a home in the clouds,

They do represent that there is a universe...

other worlds, just waiting to be explored.

That hole in the clouds, the ray of the sun,

glowing moonlight and twinkling of the stars-

They are all reminders...and a sign.

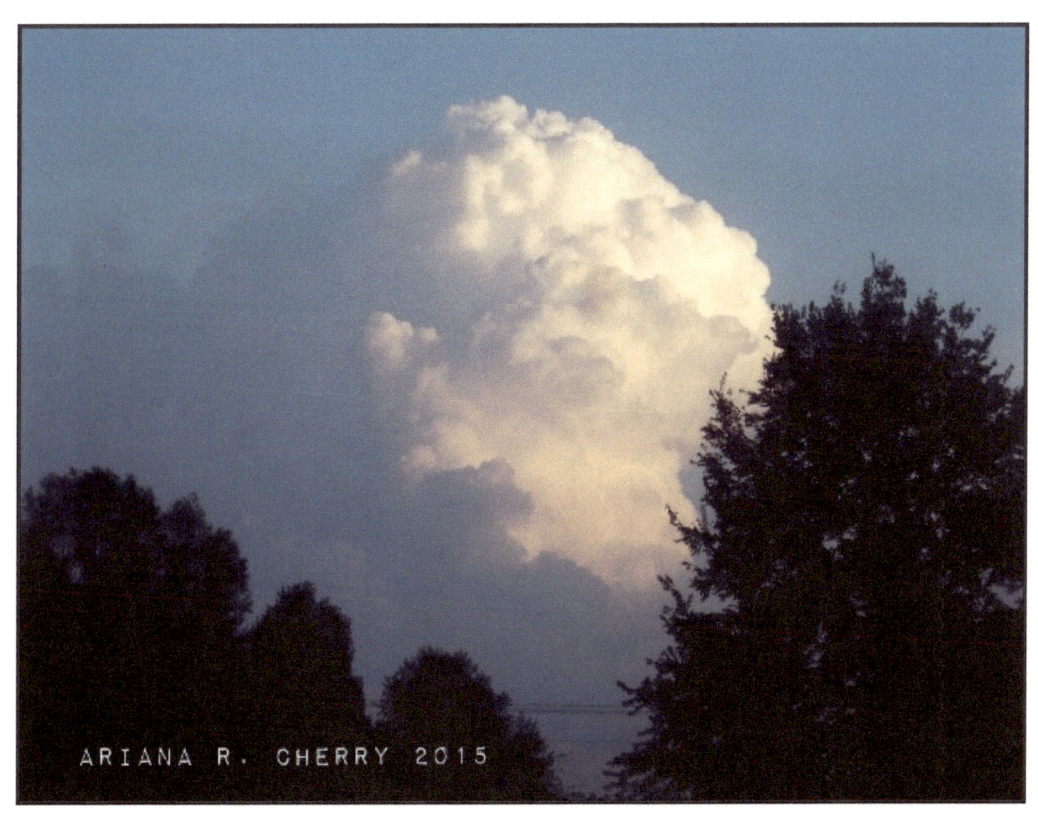

ARIANA R. CHERRY 2015

Sweet land majesties make up the
natural beauty of our Earth.
Nature is the paintings made by our creator
and they are small gifts that he presents to us everyday.

If we blink, or spend too much looking down,

We could miss these majestic moments.

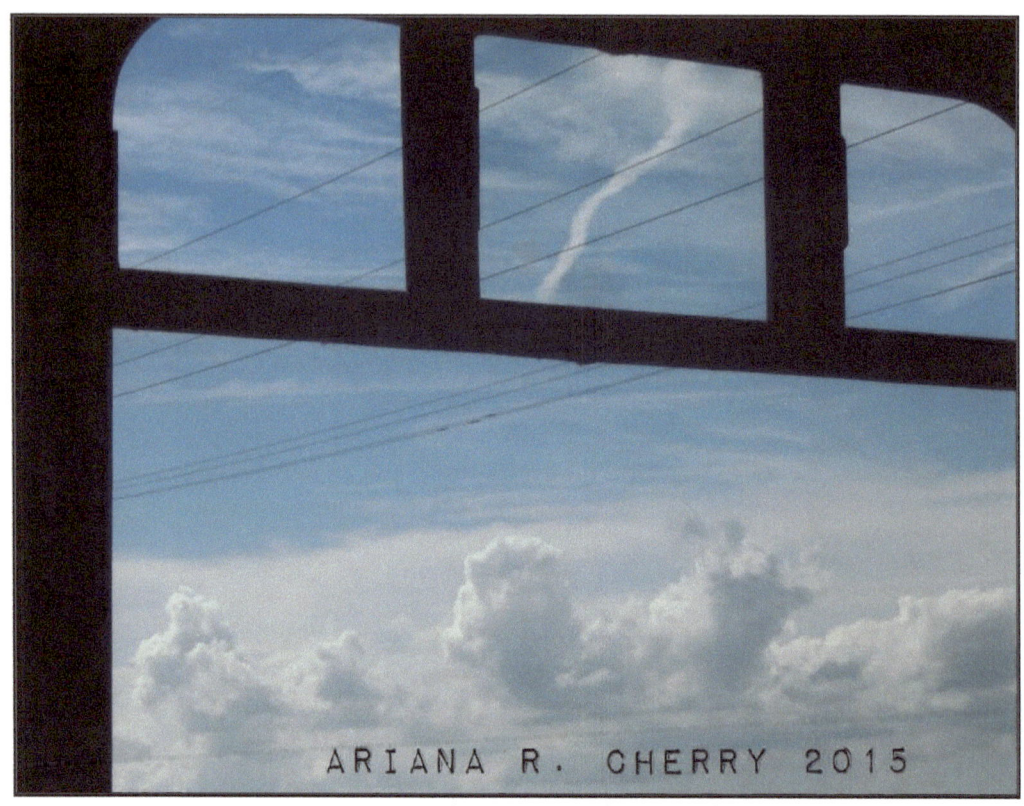

ARIANA R. CHERRY 2015

A glance out the window.

...daydreaming...

Where will the day take us?

What path will we choose?

Daydreaming of moments past...

the future...

and a hope for the current present...

It's okay to watch the roads go by

or to see the clouds float away-

Just don't miss the bus for your life's journey.

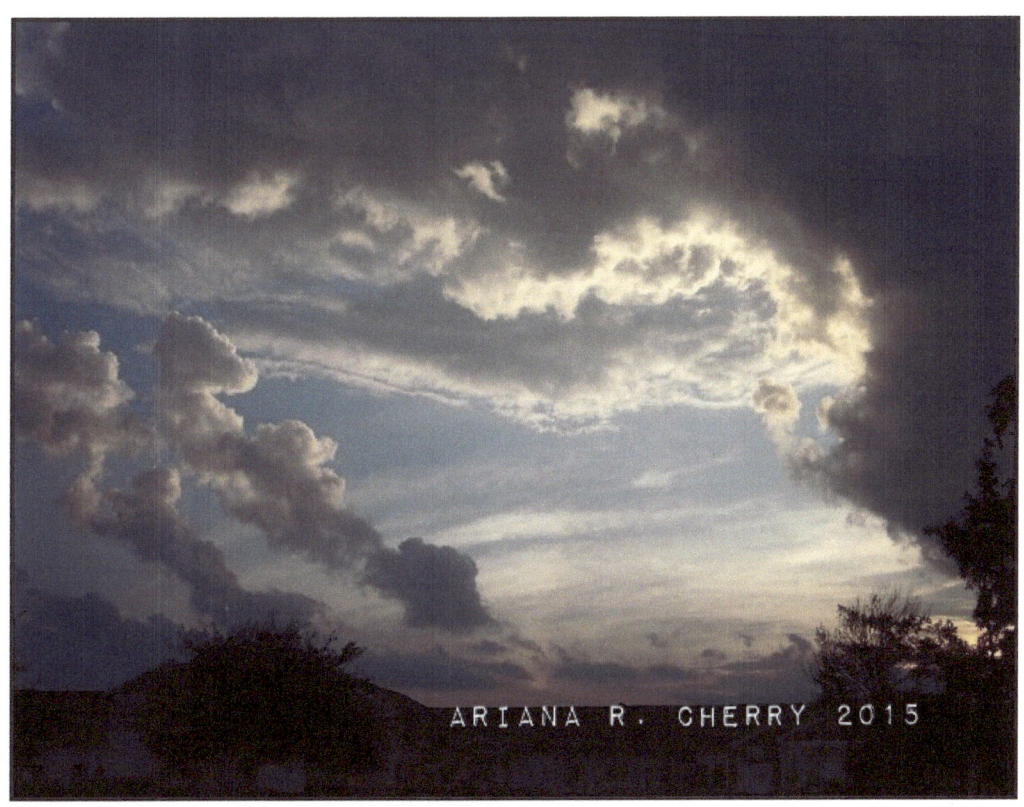

People often can get lost within themselves
And miss the beauty around them,

When they spend too much time looking down.

The world needs to lift their chin up and raise
the vail from their eyes to witness the
magnificent natural beauty
that is right in front of us.

Straight ahead, life is happening...

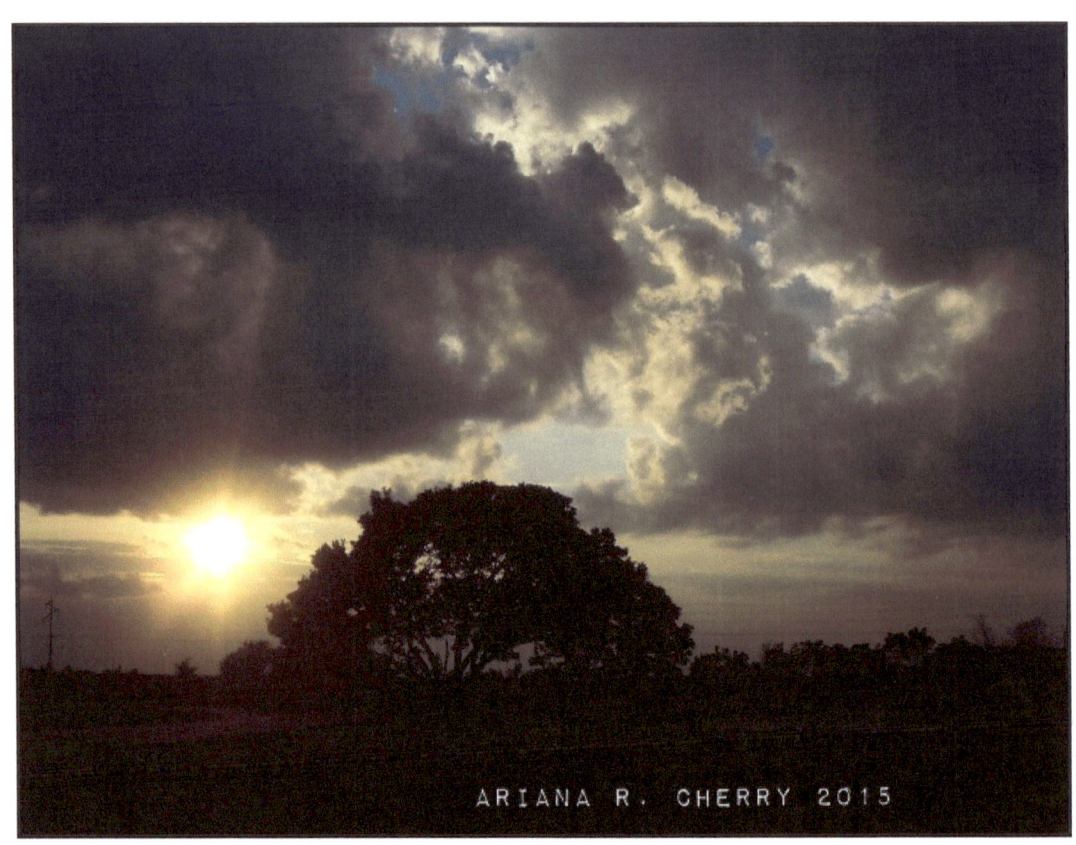

ARIANA R. CHERRY 2015

There's a special place to escape
and somewhere to get lost in our thoughts.

When we daydream,
we think back to a place
that made us feel safe...
It could be a magical world beyond the clouds,
or an escape beyond the vast universe
and high above the stars...
Another land that we may call home,

Somewhere to finally be true to ourselves.

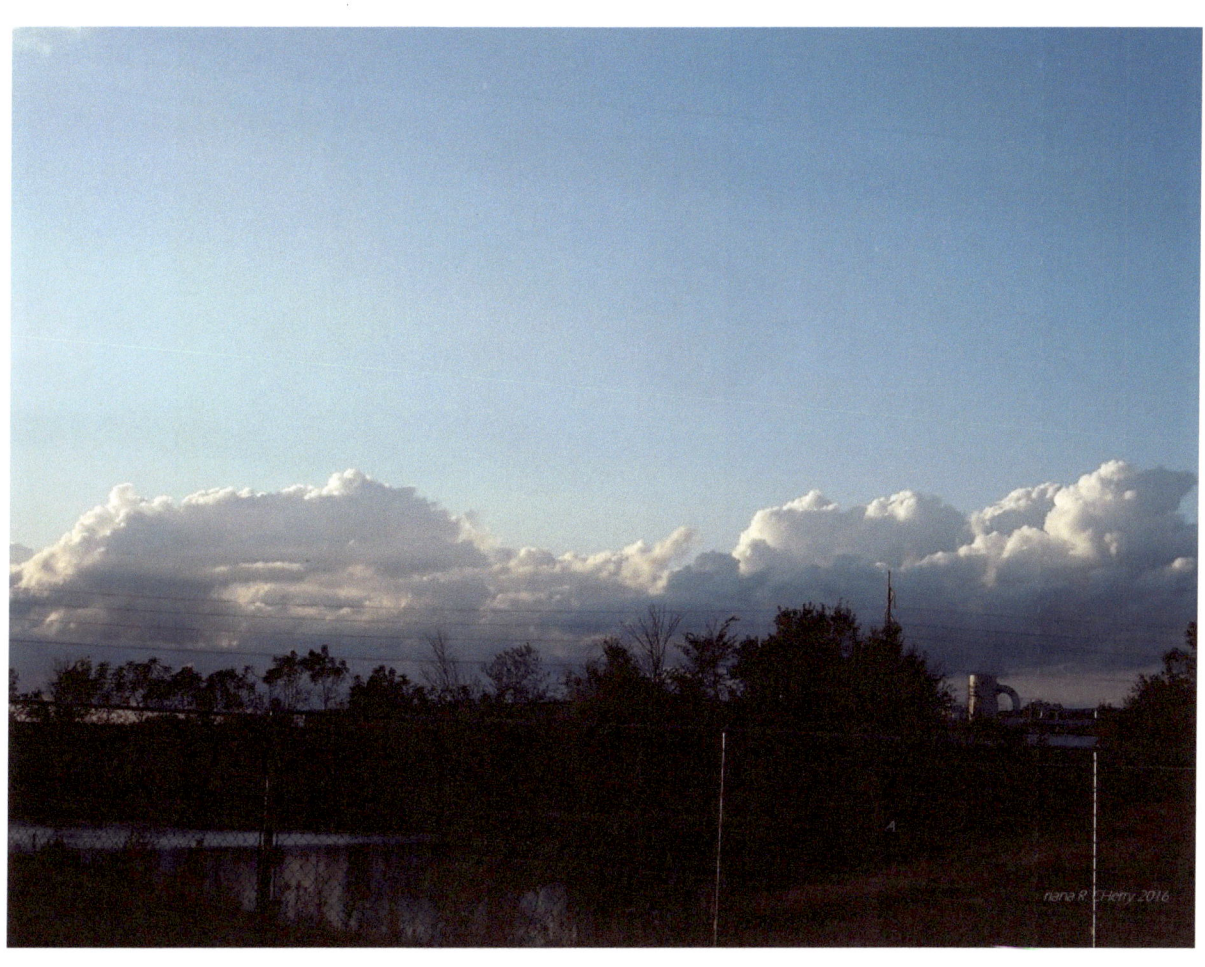

Beautiful landscapes and natural wonder
A peaceful moment and quiet get-away.
There are moments we just need silence to refresh
and gather ourselves from the noise of
our busy lives.

Sometimes, simplicity and natural beauty is all we need
and a few seconds of silence echoing from deep
within the clouds....

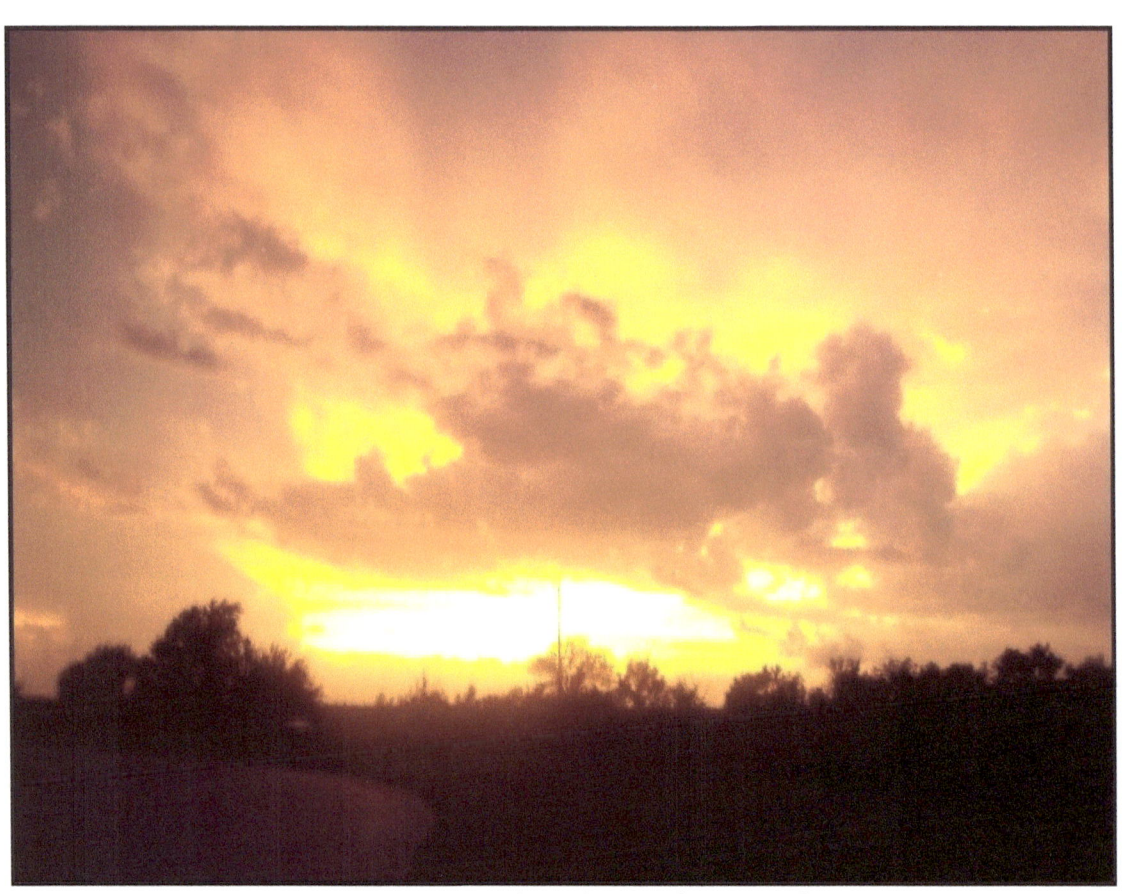

A majestic natural sunlight of golden beauty

lights up the sky.

A warmth of love radiates to the lands below.

The moment we realize love is all around us,

even if we can't see it...

It's a feeling within the beauty of nature...

the wonder we feel and appreciation

of the creation all around us.

All of this, the world, was created out of love.

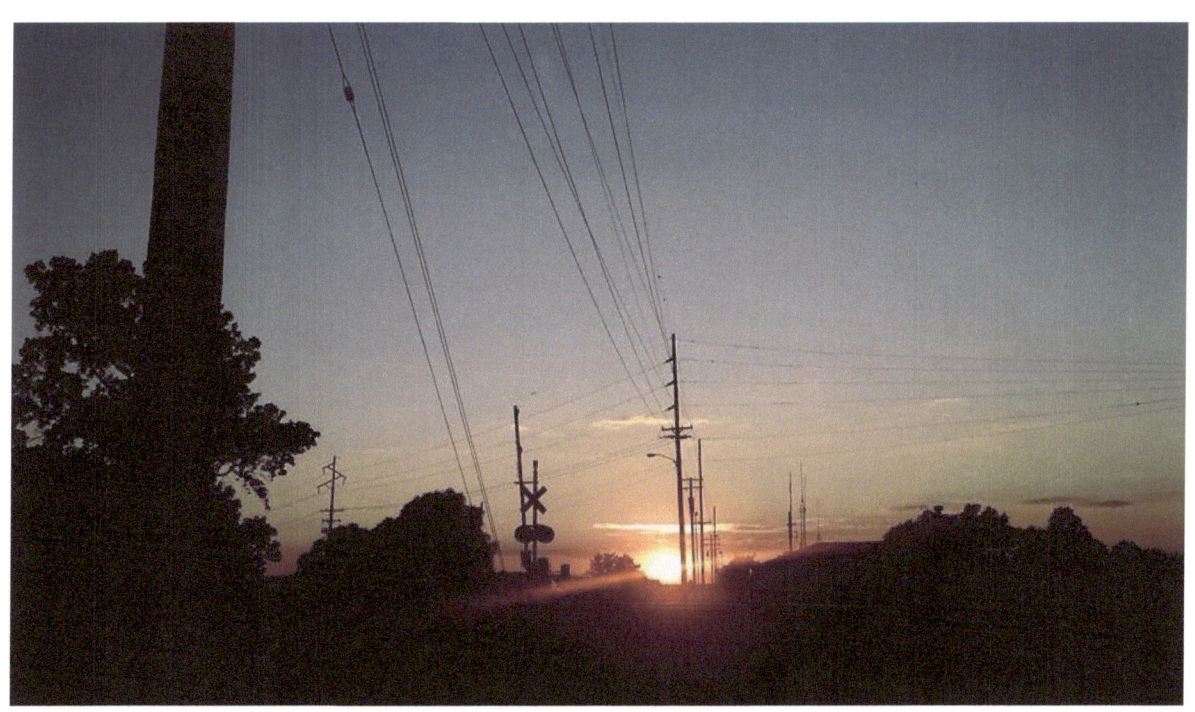

At the end of the day, we hope to go off into the sunset...
Happy ever after...

We all want a happy ending –
to make all of our dreams come true.

We wish for that glorious ride, down a winding road,
and into the sun's loving rays...

As we embark on another journey the next day.

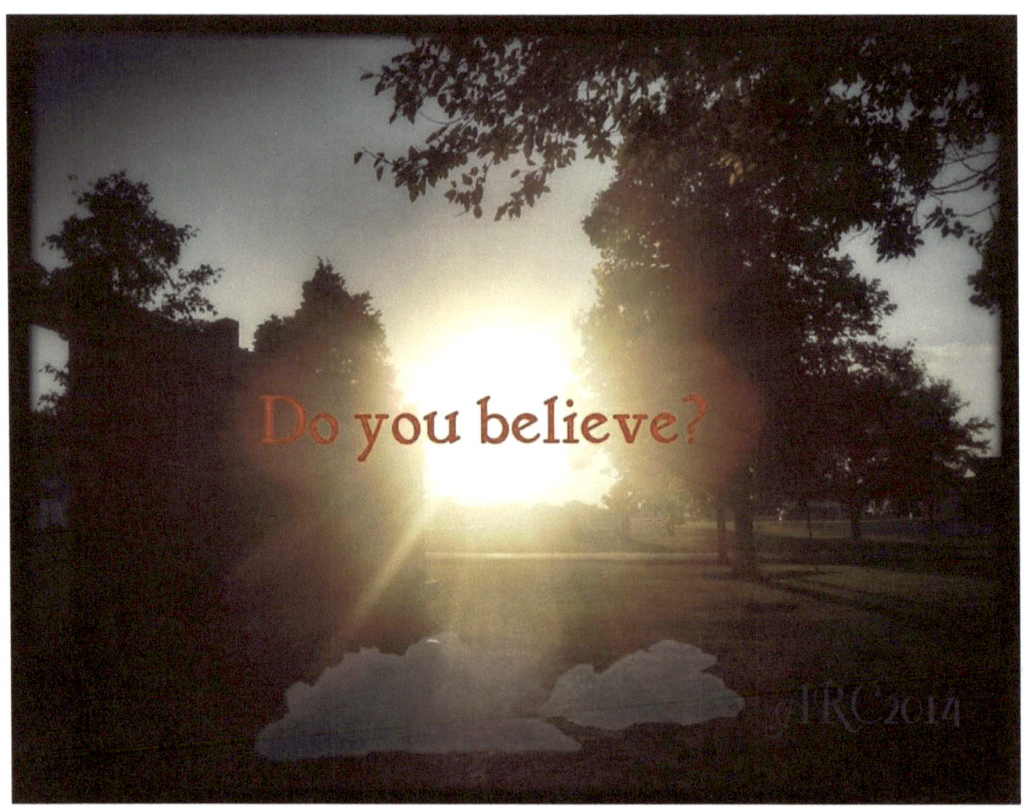

Do you believe in a higher power?

That we were meant for something
more than just this one journey?

Perhaps this is just one step –

A step into our destiny – to who we were supposed to be...

In this life – we are just beginning –

There is more yet to come...

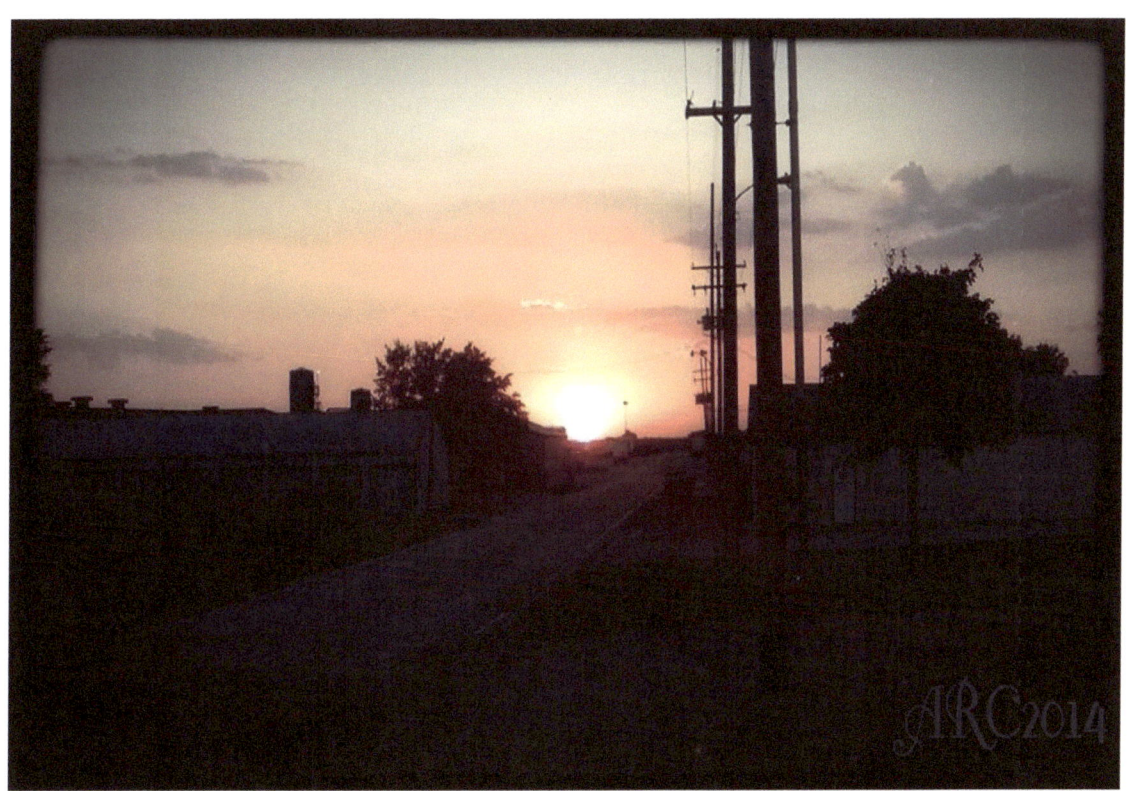

Home is where we want to end up...

We will walk into the sunset,
and to the glorious place of love.

Once we have finalized our journey, we will continue past
the sunset, beyond the stars and high above the moon.

Throughout the universe, we will fly

Until we are finally home...

About the author/photographer

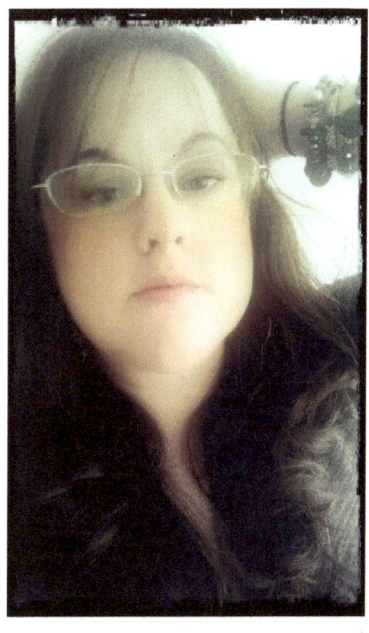

Ariana R. Cherry has been writing ever since she was a young child. She's had an interest in poetry and fictional poetry for years. As of recent, Ariana has also taken an interest in nature photography. Clouds and sunsets are some of her most favorite things to photograph. This is her first photographic collection. She thought she would make it special by mixing in some of her own inspirational writings and poetry.

Ariana has also published collections of poetry such as "The Real Me-Xtended," "Through Her Eyes," "Divine Poetry for a Spiritual Mind" and "Twisted Paths of Poetry." She also illustrated a fictional children's book, "Bullying Ben." When Ariana isn't freelance writing or taking photos, she is a reporter for a local newspaper and works as an administrative aide/secretary for a couple local churches in here area.

Stay up to date with her writing and new collections by visiting her website: http://arianarcherry.wordpress.com. You can email ariana at arianathepoet@gmail.com .

Books by Ariana R. Cherry can be purchased on
Amazon.com.

https://arianarcherry.wordpress.com/books/

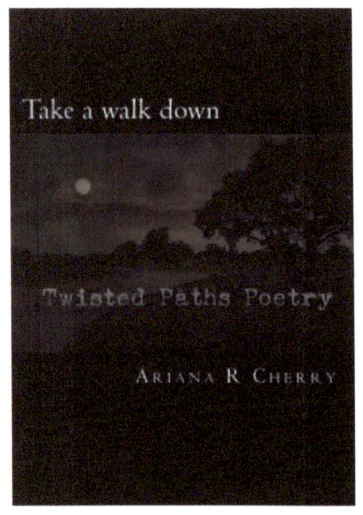
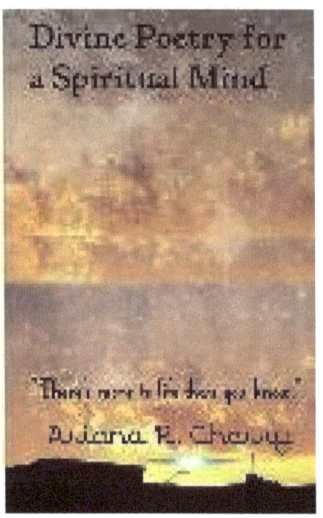
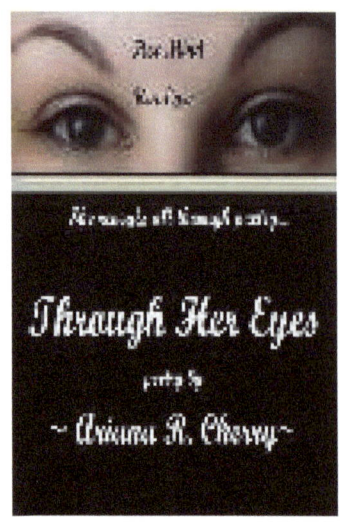

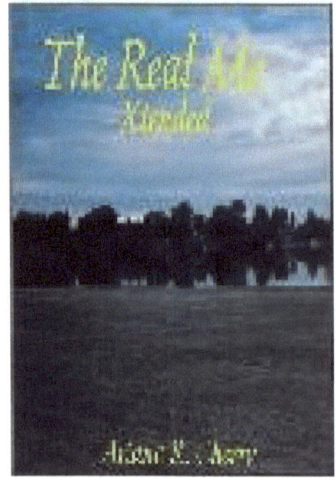
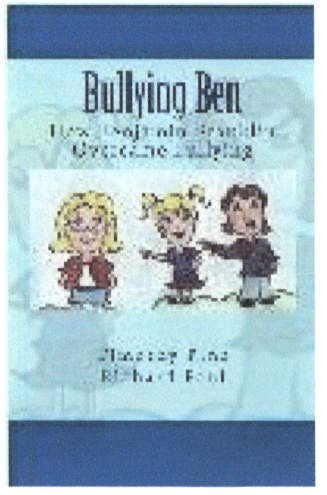

www.ingramcontent.com/pod-product-compliance
Lightning Source LLC
Chambersburg PA
CBHW041304180526

45172CB00003B/966